D0699907

Edgar, Kathleen J.
Mission San Carlos
Borromeo del Rio Carmelo
2000.
33305013140581
WO   01/06/00

Missions of California

Mission San Carlos Borromeo del Río Carmelo

Kathleen J. Edgar and Susan E. Edgar

The Rosen Publishing Group's

SANTA CLARA COUNTY LIBRARY

3 3305 01314 0581

Published in 2000 by The Rosen Publishing Group, Inc.
29 East 21st Street, New York, NY 10010

Copyright © 2000 by The Rosen Publishing Group, Inc.

All rights reserved. No part of this book may be reproduced in any form without permission in writing from the publisher, except by a reviewer.

First Edition

Book Design: Danielle Primiceri

Layout Design: Maria Melendez

Photo Credits and Illustration Credits: Pp. 1, 45 © Shirley Jordan; p. 4 © Stock Montage; pp. 5, 16, 22, 23, 25, 26, 27, 29, 30, 31, 32, 37, 39, 43, 47, 48, 50, 51 © Christina Taccone; pp. 8, 11, 13, 14 © Michael Ward; pp. 9, 12, 35, 42, 44 © SuperStock; pp. 10, 41 © Tim Hall; pp. 18, 20, 34 © CORBIS-Bettman; pp. 36, 38 © Granger Collection; pp. 52, 57 © Christine Innamorato.

Editorial Consultant Coordinator: Karen Fontanetta, M.A., Curator, Mission San Miguel Arcángel
Editorial Consultant: Ruben G. Mendoza, Ph.D., Associate Professor, Institute Director, Institute of Archaeology,
        California State University, Monterey Bay
Historical Photo Consultants: Thomas L. Davis, M.Div., M.A.
        Michael K. Ward, M.A.

Edgar, Kathleen J.
    Mission San Carlos Borromeo del Río Carmelo / by Kathleen J. Edgar and Susan E. Edgar.
        p.   cm. — (The missions of California)
    Includes bibliographical references and index.
    Summary: Discusses the founding, building, operation and closing of the Spanish Mission San Carlos in central California and its role in California history.
    ISBN 0-8239-5488-9 (lib. bdg. : alk. paper)
    1. Mission San Carlos Borromeo (Carmel, Calif.)—History—Juvenile literature. 2. Spanish mission buildings—California—Carmel Region—History—Juvenile literature. 3. Franciscans—California—Carmel Region—History—Juvenile literature. 4. California—History—To 1846—Juvenile literature. 5. Indians of North America—Missions—California—Carmel Region—History—Juvenile literature.   [1. Mission San Carlos Borromeo (Carmel, Calif.)—History. 2. Missions—California. 3. Indians of North America—California—Missions.]
    I. Edgar, Susan E. II. Title. III. Series.
    F869.M653D34   1999
    979.4'76—dc21
                                                                              99-19098
                                                                              CIP

Manufactured in the United States of America

Contents

The Spanish Explore California

In a lush valley about six miles from the Pacific Ocean, near the city of Carmel, California, lies Mission San Carlos Borromeo del Río Carmelo. Its yellowish stone walls stand out from the green hillside. Red, yellow, and purple flowers line the pathway leading to the mission's church. Centered over the entrance to the church is the Mudejar Star, a distinctive stained-glass window embedded in the rock wall.

▲ *Many people came to California in search of riches.*

The church at Mission ▶ San Carlos Borromeo.

Mission San Carlos Borromeo is a settlement built by Spanish friars (called *frays* in Spanish) and soldiers and American Indians in the 1700s. It was the second of 21 missions founded by the Spanish along the coast of the Pacific Ocean between 1769 and 1823. The missions were intended to bring the Christian religion to the American Indians and to increase the size and wealth of the Spanish empire.

Spain's interest in this land began after Christopher Columbus reached the New World (Spain's name for what we now call South America, Central America, and North America) in 1492. Spain was a world power at that time. The Spanish government sent men to explore the lands of the New World in search of riches, including gold. The Spanish wanted to claim these new lands and any resources there as their own, making them property of the Spanish empire.

Most Spanish citizens were Roman Catholics. They believed in Christianity (the teachings of the Bible and Jesus Christ). There were many Indians living in the New World, and the Spanish wanted to teach them about Christianity. The Catholics believed only Christians went to heaven after death, so they thought it was in the best interest of the Indians to give up their religion and become Christians.

The First Expedition to Alta California

In 1602, the Spanish government sent Sebastián Vizcaíno to Alta California. At the time, "California" mostly described what is now the state of California and the Baja Peninsula of Mexico. The Baja Peninsula was known as Baja (meaning "lower") California, while today's state of California was known as Alta (meaning "upper")

California (although Alta California's boundaries were not the same as California's are today).

Vizcaíno discovered Monterey Bay (near Carmel) and claimed the land for the Spanish empire. Members of the expedition went ashore and held a Catholic Mass (church service) under an oak tree. Vizcaíno's party named the area Carmel after Mt. Carmel in the Holy Land (now part of Israel). In his writings, Vizcaíno described Monterey as "the best port that could be desired…it has many pines…and live oaks and white oaks, and water in great quantity, all near the shore."

○ San Francisco de Solano
○ San Rafael Arcángel
○ San Francisco de Asís
○ San José

○ Santa Clara de Asís
○ Santa Cruz
○ San Juan Bautista
○ San Carlos Borromeo del Río Carmelo
○ Nuestra Señora de la Soledad

○ San Antonio de Padua
○ San Miguel Arcángel

○ San Luis Obispo de Tolosa

○ La Purísima Concepción
○ Santa Inés
○ Santa Bárbara
○ San Buenaventura

○ San Fernando Rey de España
○ San Gabriel Arcángel

○ San Juan Capistrano

○ San Luis Rey de Francia

○ San Diego de Alcalá

This map shows where the Alta California missions were founded. ▶

The Esselen Indians

When explorer Vizcaíno visited Alta California, more than 300,000 Indians lived there. The Indians lived in villages of between 80 and 100 people belonging to the same group, or tribe. Each tribe considered certain areas of land as its own. Sometimes tribes would fight over land rights.

Many of the Indians who lived near Carmel were known as the Esselen. They lived in villages and built cone-shaped houses using grass, bark, plank, and brush bundled together.

Hunters and Gatherers

The Esselen had a lot of personal freedom. They were nomadic, which meant that they moved their homes from time to time. If one area became low on water, food, building supplies, or firewood, they built new villages in a more plentiful area.

The Esselen hunted and gathered their food. Their diet included animals, plants, nuts, and insects. The men were hunters and fishermen. They used bows and arrows, traps, spears, and nets to hunt game and catch fish. Their diet included bear cubs, deer, rodents, birds, fish, sardines, rabbits, ducks, and sea creatures. The Esselen men made tools and weapons from materials they could find near their villages, such as wood, grass, shells, bone, and stone. The Esselen also wove nets out of long-stemmed grass or reeds they

◀ *Esselen Indians and their huts.*

▲
The Esselen used arrows and spears to hunt.

9

Esselen fisherman.

found growing near the water.

The Esselen women were responsible for gathering food and cooking. They collected grass, bulbs, seeds, herbs, roots, acorns, berries, and nuts. Acorns were a major source of nutrition for the Indians. Women used mortars and pestles made from stones to grind the acorns into flour for bread, mush, and cakes. Because acorns are poisonous and can cause sickness or even death, the women had to leach the acorn flour (wash it with water) at least 10 times before it was safe to eat. Women made baskets for leaching, cooking, storing food, and carrying water.

Esselen men and women wore few clothes in the warm California climate. In fact, the men often went naked. Women wore apronlike skirts made of bark, grass, or hides. In cooler weather, they wore blankets made of animal fur. They had ceremonial outfits that were worn for special events. Some Indians, especially women, tattooed their faces. Many Esselen had pierced ears in which they wore small

Indian women collected grass in clay bowls.

sticks or carved wood or stone ornaments. Some Esselen painted their bodies for decoration.

The Esselen Way of Life

Nature played an important role in the Esselen's religion. They respected all things. Animals, plants, people, and the land all held special significance in their culture. They believed in a creator as well as other gods and spirits. The spirits were at work in their environment and often took the forms of things in nature, such as the sun, moon, and wind. Some spirits did good deeds, while others brought about hardship and illness. Medicine men, called shamans, used herbs and other remedies to heal the sick.

An Esselen Indian medicine man.

Esselen life was full of ceremonies that included singing and dancing. Such rituals marked the beginning of hunting trips and warfare. Weddings and births were celebrated, and the dead were honored. Initiation ceremonies brought both boys and girls into adulthood.

The Esselen lived this way for hundreds of years. Their way of life was to be changed forever by the arrival of the Spanish and the establishment of Mission San Carlos Borromeo.

The Mission System

Long before the founding of Mission San Carlos Borromeo, the Spanish began colonizing the New World. During the 1500s, the Spanish built missions in New Spain (today's Mexico). They established a capital in Mexico City. The Spanish wanted the American Indians living in New Spain to adopt the Spanish lifestyle, language, and religion. They came from a world that looked down on the Indians. The Spanish thought the Indians were uncivilized because they were not educated in schools, wore few clothes, lived off of the land, and moved from place to place. The Spanish thought that it was in the best interest of the Indians to live as Spaniards instead of as the "savages" the Spanish perceived them to be.

▲
A picture of a friar teaching Indians about religion.

12

The friars needed the Indians' help to ▶ build the mission.

The Spanish wanted the Indians to help them ranch and farm at the missions.

By the 1700s, the Spanish government had procedures for building religious settlements, called missions, in New Spain. Soldiers and

14

missionaries were sent to teach the Indians about Spanish practices and Christianity. In addition, the missionaries trained the Indians in how to grow food, raise cattle and sheep, and make tools and crafts such as soap, candles, horseshoes, and woven and leather goods. Also, the friars instructed the Indians in Christian beliefs. In the meantime, the soldiers began building presidios (fortresses) to guard the land they had claimed for Spain against other countries who also wanted it.

The Spanish estimated that it would take 10 years to train the Indians in Spanish work methods. After this time, the Spanish intended to return the mission lands to the Indians to operate by themselves. The land would still belong to Spain, and the Indians would become tax-paying Spanish citizens. This process was called secularization. Once the lands were returned to the Indians, the missionaries would travel to another area, build a new mission, and teach other Indians about the Spanish way of life and religion.

By the 1700s, the Spanish had built many missions in what we now consider Central and South America as well as in New Spain. They became fearful that they would lose Alta California to settlers from England and Russia, so they quickly started a chain of missions in that area.

The Founders of Mission
San Carlos Borromeo del Río Carmelo

The government of New Spain sent land and sea expeditions to Alta California in 1769, under the command of Captain Don Gaspár de Portolá, governor of the Californias. His task was to assist Fray Junípero Serra in starting the chain of missions. These two men led the other missionaries and the California Indians in the establishment of Mission San Carlos Borromeo.

Fray Serra

Fray Serra was born on November 24, 1713, in Petra de Majorca, Spain. He became a priest in 1737 and taught philosophy at schools in his homeland. Because he was a skilled teacher and preacher, and because he believed strongly in the Christian faith, he came to New Spain as a missionary.

When he was in his mid-50s, Serra was chosen by Roman Catholic Church officials to be the president of the mission system planned for Alta California. His first task as the head of this project was to begin building the first two missions in the wilderness of Alta California. He was almost too sick to make the trip due to a severe leg infection caused by an insect bite, but he traveled 750 miles to the first mission location despite his illness.

During his 15 years in Alta California, Serra founded nine missions and baptized more than 6,000 California Indians. As mission president, Serra made his headquarters at Carmel but traveled frequently to check on the other missions. He died in 1784. Sailors, soldiers, settlers, friars, and more than 600 Indians attended his funeral. Fray Francisco Palóu wrote that the mission bells announced Serra's

Many statues throughout California honor Serra's memory.

17

A baptism of California Indians.

passing: "[T]he whole town assembled, weeping over the death of their beloved father." Today, Serra is a candidate for Catholic sainthood, an honor given to those in the Catholic faith who have devoted their lives to God.

Captain Portolá

Captain Don Gaspár de Portolá was a Spanish noble, born in Balageur, Spain, in 1723. After many successful years in the military,

18

he was named governor of the Californias. He led the expeditions to San Diego and Monterey and worked with Serra to begin the Alta California missions. After Portolá established the mission in Monterey in 1770, he returned to New Spain. In 1777, he became mayor of Puebla, New Spain.

Fray Juan Crespí

Portolá and Serra's expedition included soldiers, settlers, Christian Indians from New Spain, and several friars. One of the friars was Fray Juan Crespí. Crespí was born in Majorca and was a student of Serra's for a time. While on the journey to San Diego, Crespí served as the group's diarist, recording the details of their journey. A lifelong friend of Serra's, Crespí died at the age of 60 on January 1, 1782, in Carmel. Fray Crespí was buried in the mission church sanctuary.

The Journey to Alta California

Five expeditions left Mexico to set up missions in Alta California in 1769. Three ships sailed northward along the Pacific coast. Two land expeditions traveled across the rough desert terrain of Baja California. All expeditions were to meet near the harbor in San Diego.

The journey was difficult for everyone. Many of the ships' crew members got sick along the way and some died. Some developed scurvy, a disease caused by a lack of fresh fruits and vegetables. One ship was lost at sea.

The land expeditions didn't fare any better. They brought many things with them to start the missions. The friars had received money

▲

Captain Gaspar de Portolá.

from the government of New Spain to buy supplies, tools, and religious artifacts, including bells for the church and vestments. Missions in New Spain provided cattle and sheep.

By the time the explorers and ships met at San Diego, less than half of the 219 men who had started out on the journey were still alive. Once there, Fray Serra and some of the soldiers, sailors, and Christian Indians that had journeyed with him started to clear land for Mission San Diego de Alcalá, the first of the California missions. On July 14, 1769, Portolá and about 65 men left in search of Monterey—the spot that had been described by Vizcaíno back in 1602.

Their first efforts to find Vizcaíno's Monterey Bay were unrewarded.

The expedition reached the area on October 1, 1769, but the landscape didn't match Vizcaíno's description, and the explorers weren't certain they had found it. Upon arrival, Portolá described his band as "skeletons who had been spared by scurvy, hunger, and thirst." After more searching, the tired and hungry crew headed back to San Diego, disheartened. They left a cross near the bay with the inscription "the overland expedition from San Diego returned from this place...starving."

On January 24, 1770, Portolá's expedition arrived back in San Diego, six months after they had left. He found that resources were dangerously low in San Diego and sent Captain Rivera on a ship called the *San Antonio* to Baja California for more supplies.

Portolá's group waited and waited for Rivera's return. They planned to leave San Diego if supplies didn't arrive soon. Fray Serra asked Portolá for more time and began to pray. A day before they were to leave, the *San Antonio* was spotted on the horizon. Captain Rivera returned loaded with supplies for the explorers.

With new provisions to sustain the group, the search for Monterey could continue. After traveling for about a month, Portolá's group found the cross it had erected on its last trip to Monterey several months earlier. Now, though, the cross was covered with offerings of meat, fish, sardines, arrows, and feathers. The Esselen had left these gifts to acknowledge the hard times that the expedition had endured. Upon their return to the area, the Spaniards traded ribbons and beads with the Indians in return for piñon nuts, venison (deer meat), and other foods.

Fray Serra and the *San Antonio* arrived at the port one week later. The group chose to build Mission San Carlos Borromeo del Río

The missionaries brought bells to use in the church.

Carmelo near a large oak tree that they believed Vizcaíno's group had used for religious services back in 1602. On June 3, 1770, with the Esselen watching in the distance, the Spanish hung a bell in the oak tree, and Mass was conducted by Fray Serra. A statue of the Virgin Mary (the mother of Jesus) was placed on an altar made of logs. All the members of the group participated in raising a cross and a Spanish flag. Muskets and cannons were fired during the dedication of the new mission.

Portolá returned to New Spain aboard the *San Antonio*. When he delivered the news of the founding of the first two missions (Mission San Carlos Borromeo and Mission San Diego de Alcalá) to the officials in Mexico City, church bells rang throughout New Spain signaling its success. Fray Serra had stayed behind in California.

▲ *Statue of the Virgin Mary.*

◀ *Church bells played an important role in mission life.*

23

The Beginnings of Mission
San Carlos Borromeo del Río Carmelo

Building the Mission

In 1770, as construction of the mission began in Monterey, Fray Serra and the other settlers knew that this was not the best site for a settlement. The soil was poor, and few Esselen lived close by. Within the first year, Serra received permission from the government of New Spain to find a better site. He chose an area six miles to the south in the Carmel Valley, close to the sea. However, because of Monterey's strategic location on the Pacific coast, the army continued to build the presidio, or military fort, there and the mission at Carmel. They believed that this was the best way to protect the area from the threat of other European settlers trying to take the land away from Spain.

The Presidio at Monterey

Miguel Costansó, a military engineer and architect, had accompanied Serra and Portolá on their expedition to set up missions at San Diego and Monterey. Costansó's plan was to build a 200-square-foot presidio. Living quarters, a warehouse, a storage room for gun powder, and other buildings would be constructed within the presidio.

In one month's time, workers who had come to Alta California with the missionaries built a rough stockade out of dirt and logs. Many cannons were placed in the walls to protect the presidio from a sea invasion.

A storeroom was used for religious services until a church could be built. Friars traveled from Carmel to Monterey to conduct religious services for the soldiers and settlers living at the presidio. In 1794, La Capilla Real, the Royal Presidio Chapel, was dedicated in

The church at Mission San Carlos Borromeo. ▶

▲

The mission church had its own kitchen.

Monterey. It remains the oldest continuously used church in California today.

The Mission at Carmel

Before beginning construction of the mission, Serra blessed the land of the Carmel Valley, calling it the "Garden of God." He held Mass on August 24, 1771, and officially dedicated Mission San Carlos Borromeo del Río Carmelo. Then the group set about constructing the mission buildings.

All the mission complexes in Alta California needed to meet standards set by the Spanish government. Each mission was to be like a small city, built in a quadrangle (square or rectangle). In the center was a courtyard, called a garth or patio. Around the garth were living quarters, storerooms, work rooms, a kitchen, and a dining room. The friars' quarters were called the *convento*. A church or chapel was constructed in the northeast corner. A wall surrounded the buildings like a fortress. Fields for grazing cattle and sheep were outside of the mission's

▲
The dining room at Mission San Carlos Borromeo.

walls. Other fields were used for planting and harvesting crops.

Missions varied in size. On the average, a mission controlled about 500 square miles of land. Some missions were so large that *asistencias* (branch churches) were built many miles away. The *asistencia* had a chapel, living quarters, and work rooms. This allowed the missionaries to teach Indians that were far away from the main mission. In addition to *asistencias*, missions often had *rancherías* (small ranches with stables and corrals). The *ranchería* also allowed the *vaqueros* (cowboys or ranch hands) to tend to the animals that grazed far from the mission. Mission San Carlos Borromeo would eventually have two *rancherías*: Buena Vista and El Tucho.

The first structures at Mission San Carlos Borromeo were made with log walls and thatched roofs. There were 5 sailors, 3 soldiers, and 40

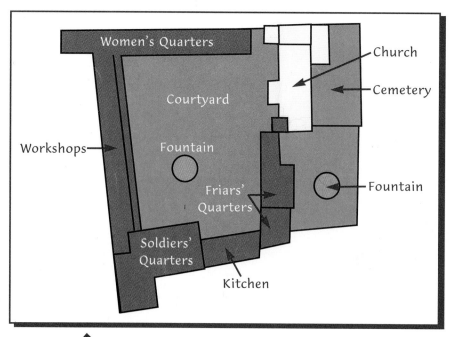

The design, or floor plan of the mission.

A wall carving showing Serra working with Esselen Indians.

Christian Indians from Baja California working on these buildings. Within six months, the laborers had constructed a wooden chapel, living quarters, a storehouse, and a corral within a wooden stockade.

The First Stages

The Esselen Indians watched as the laborers gathered the materials needed to build the mission complex. The workers cut down trees using axes and saws made of metal. The Esselen had never seen tools like these before. Some of the Esselen were curious to try the new Spanish tools and offered to help the newcomers. Once the Indians expressed an interest, the missionaries and soldiers seized the opportunity to put them to work and taught them how to use the tools.

Finishing the Mission

When the construction of

Tools used by the Indians to help build the mission.

This structure is made from adobe.

Mission San Carlos Borromeo was well underway, Fray Serra set out to establish more missions in Alta California. Although he set up his headquarters in Carmel, he traveled frequently to the other mission sites. He put Fray Francisco Palóu, another of his former students, in charge of Mission San Carlos Borromeo. Palóu oversaw the construction of many more buildings and workshops between 1771 and 1784.

Most of the structures were made of wood, but several, such as the kitchen, storerooms, and carpentry shop, were made of adobe bricks. Adobe is a mixture of clay, water, straw, and sometimes manure. It was packed into molds to make bricks. The bricks were then dried in the sun.

An irrigation ditch was dug to bring fresh water from the Carmel River to Mission San Carlos Borromeo. At the end of the ditch, the workers dug a large pool to trap fish for food.

Fray Serra died in 1784. When Fray Palóu retired the following year, Fray Fermín Francisco Lasuén took over leadership of the mission. He later became the new president of the Alta California missions.

In 1791, Manuel Ruíz, a master mason from New Spain, was commissioned to build a new church to replace Mission San Carlos Borromeo's first one. Ruíz chose to build the new church on the same

site as the original church, where both Fray Serra and Fray Crespí were buried. By 1793, the building of the new church began with the help of Lasuén and the other residents of the mission.

For the church, large yellowish-orange slabs of sandstone were quarried from the nearby Santa Lucia

▲

Fray Serra's coffin.

Mountains. They were hauled to the Carmel Valley on *carretas* (wooden carts pulled by oxen or mules). The laborers created an arched ceiling 33 feet high and covered the walls with a plaster made from seashells. The floor was made from clay tiles that were burned in a hot oven. After four years of work, the church was completed in 1797.

◀ *The plaster on this mission wall has started to chip away.*

Daily Life at the Mission

The friars and soldiers at Mission San Carlos Borromeo and its presidio were far away from home without many of the comforts they had once known. Fray Serra's room at Mission San Carlos Borromeo was similar to the rooms of other missionaries. It was rustic, with only a wooden cot, coarse blanket, chest, table, chair, and candle. The missionaries and other settlers often felt isolated. They didn't have much contact with people who had the same background as they did. They had trouble communicating with the Esselen since the Esselen language was much different from Spanish.

The missionaries taught the Esselen about the Catholic religion and European agriculture, trades, ranching, and cooking. They encouraged the Esselen to work on the mission by offering them food and trinkets. The friars taught Bible lessons, conducted Mass, and performed baptisms, weddings, and funerals. They also tried to maintain good relations with Spanish military and government officials, since problems often arose over the treatment of the Indians and other issues about how to run the mission.

Missionaries kept annual records that were later stored at Mission San Carlos Borromeo. They recorded facts about things like agricultural production, livestock holdings, and the number of Indians who had converted to Christianity. The records show that in 1784, Mission San Carlos Borromeo harvested nearly 63,300 pounds of wheat, 72,000 pounds of corn, and 70,000 pounds of barley. In 1795, more than 875 neophytes lived at the mission. By 1834 the number had dwindled to 165.

Life at Mission San Carlos Borromeo was very regimented. The friars

Serra's bedroom at Mission San Carlos Borromeo.

were accustomed to rigorous discipline and expected the same from the neophytes. The Esselen were required to work most of the day and learn to follow Catholic practices that had little or nothing to do with their own beliefs or lifestyle. Many Esselen had trouble adjusting.

▲

This drawing shows a Catholic conversion ceremony.

A Typical Day at Mission San Carlos Borromeo

Bells rang to wake mission residents around sunrise. Everyone assembled in the garth and headed to the church for morning Mass, prayers, and instruction in Christian beliefs. Breakfast was cooked by the women neophytes. The Indians ate *atole*, a mush of corn or grain.

Next, work assignments were given to the Esselen adults, while Esselen children attended lessons. The Spanish showed the Esselen men and women European work methods. They taught the men how to grow crops such as corn, wheat, and beans. The men were also trained to be carpenters, blacksmiths, makers of adobe tiles and bricks, shepherds, and *vaqueros* who herded cattle. They worked to repair the mission and construct new buildings.

The Spanish instructed neophyte women in cooking, particularly how to cook in brick ovens. Eventually corn and wheat flour were used instead of acorn flour. The women learned to use Spanish looms to make clothing and blankets for everyone in the mission. They crafted

34

Many Indian rituals involved singing and dancing.

soap from tallow (fat from cattle that is melted, then allowed to cool and harden).

At midday, lunch, usually consisting of *pozole* (a stew made of barley, beans, vegetables, and meat), was served. After lunch, everyone enjoyed a *siesta* (a time to rest or nap) before returning to work. Another Mass was held late in the afternoon. Supper was followed by prayers, Bible teachings, and Spanish-language lessons. In the evening, the Esselen had some time for recreation. The Indians liked to sing, dance, and play games of chance.

The routine of daily life was broken on occasion when *fiestas* (feast days) were held for births, weddings, or other celebrations. The Esselen ceremonies featured the traditional songs and dances of their heritage. The missionaries usually didn't stop the Indians from conducting traditional ceremonies, even though such rituals contradicted Christian beliefs. The friars allowed these ceremonies so that the Indians' frustration with being at the mission wouldn't build, and they would remain peaceful.

The Esselen often used leisure time from mission tasks to play games.

The Hardships of Mission Life

The Spanish and California Indian cultures often clashed at the mission. For the Esselen, mission life was difficult. The daily schedule was very strictly enforced by the missionaries and soldiers. The Esselen were expected to adjust to the Spanish ways. Many had trouble with the regimented lifestyle and wanted to leave the mission. Once they converted to Christianity and lived at the mission, though, they were not permitted to leave. Though the mission gates were bolted shut, some Indians did manage to escape, but they were chased, brought back to the mission, and punished by flogging. Because of the friars' religious beliefs, they felt it was necessary to lock the single women in their dormitories at night. Many of the Esselen felt they had been brought into mission life against their wills and resented the missionaries and soldiers.

▲
An Indian being beaten for disobedience.

Some of the Spanish soldiers at Mission San Carlos Borromeo treated the Esselen badly, abusing the Indian women and beating some men to death.

In the 1770s, Fray Serra traveled to New Spain to talk to government officials about the problem of soldiers mistreating mission Indians. Serra returned to Alta California

A Christian reliquary, or shrine. ▶

with a document from the Spanish government stating that the missionaries could take control of the Indians away from the military. This document is considered a Native American Bill of Rights, even though many soldiers disregarded the order and continued the cruelty.

Nature's Trials

The first winter in the Carmel Valley was very harsh. There wasn't enough food at the mission. A band of soldiers traveled south in search of food. Their efforts were rewarded near an area known as

◀ *Fray Serra.*

Obispo, the Valley of the Bears. The soldiers brought back enough bear meat to last until spring.

Although the residents of the mission planted crops of wheat, corn, and barley each spring, the harvests didn't produce enough food to keep Mission San Carlos Borromeo thriving in its early years. Ships found it difficult to deliver supplies to the coastal mission because of unpredictable weather and storms. By 1774, Don Juan Bautista de Anza established an overland route, which allowed supplies to travel on a regular basis from New Spain to Alta California. Meanwhile, other missions came to the aid of Mission San

A sign dedicated to Don Juan Bautista. ▶

Carlos Borromeo, supplying bushels of wheat, beans, and corn.

Sickness and Death

Disease was another problem facing California Indians. For the first time, they were exposed to European diseases, such as measles, smallpox, chicken pox, and syphilis. Although these diseases were rarely fatal to the Spaniards, the Indians' bodies had not developed any resistance to them. Many of the Indians throughout Alta California became sick and died from European diseases that their immune systems were not equipped to fight off.

The neophytes' living conditions also caused disease. Women neophytes were locked in overcrowded, unclean dormitories. Poor ventilation and improper sanitation systems contributed to the problem, making many of the Indians sick and attracting bugs and rats.

Pirate Raid of 1818

In October 1818, the mission was raided by pirates. Several ships, led by the pirate Hippolyte de Bouchard, sat off the coast in Monterey harbor. The ships began firing upon the presidio, but the Spanish soldiers fought back. They forced the pirates to surrender and flee out to sea. Then the pirates made an attack on foot. The small band of Spanish soldiers at the presidio ran, as 400 pirates captured the presidio's cannons. The missionaries and neophytes evacuated the mission. Bouchard and his men looted the presidio and set fire to the fortress, but they left Mission San Carlos Borromeo intact.

Many Indians on the mission became sick and died.

MAP
OF
CALIFORNIA
NEW MEXICO TEXAS &c
Published by H. S. Tanner No 156 Fulton St
NEW YORK
1849.

SCALE

Secularization

While life at Mission San Carlos Borromeo was difficult, there was also trouble brewing in New Spain. In 1810, a civil war broke out in what would soon be considered Mexico. After 11 years of fighting, Mexico gained independence from Spain in 1821, and the missions in Alta California fell under the authority of the Mexican government.

The newly independent Mexicans had different ideas about the missions than the Spanish had. They believed that the Indians living at the missions were being treated like slaves. In 1826, the Mexican government passed laws to emancipate (free) the Indians. Although they were now free to leave the missions, many of the Esselen were so used to mission life that they were afraid to go.

Fray José Reál arrived to oversee operations at Mission San Carlos Borromeo in 1833. In August of that same year, secularization laws finally went into effect in California. Originally the Spanish had planned to secularize the missions after 10 years of operation. However, the friars had kept control of the missions rather than secularizing them. They believed that the Indians still needed guidance in the ways of the Spanish religion and culture and were not ready to run the missions on their own.

Though secularization was intended to distribute the mission lands, buildings, and livestock to the neophytes, most of the mission lands ended up in the hands of Mexican and Spanish landowners.

◀ *The coat of arms.*

◀ *Map of Alta California.*

▲
Sutter was the first man to discover gold in California.

instead. In fact, so much of the land became privately owned that the Catholics eventually had to buy back a section of land in front of the church at Mission San Carlos Borromeo to allow people to enter through the front doors without trespassing on privately owned land.

Many Esselen left Mission San Carlos Borromeo and moved into the community surrounding the presidio at Monterey, becoming *vaqueros* or ranch hands.

Mexico's hold on Alta California lasted only a few years. American settlers from the East began moving into the area. In the late 1840s, miners discovered gold in California and thousands of settlers rushed there hoping to find riches. Soon enough, the United States government decided that it would like to own the land of Alta California and began to fight with Mexico over control of it. Finally, in 1850, Alta California became part of the United States and was renamed California. The land now belonged to the United States government.

In the 1850s, the U.S. Federal Land Commission returned sections

Roofing tools used to repair the church roof.

of the mission lands to the Roman Catholic Church. The church, *convento*, and several other buildings at Mission San Carlos Borromeo were returned to the Catholic Church by United States president James Buchanan in 1859. By that time, the church roof had collapsed, exposing the interior walls to the weather, and the church became a sanctuary for birds, squirrels, cattle, and other wildlife.

The Legacy of Mission
San Carlos Borromeo del Río Carmelo

Restoration

During the 1880s, in anticipation of the 100-year anniversary of Fray Serra's death, missionaries began restoration efforts at Mission San Carlos Borromeo. Father Angel Casanova commissioned a shingle roof to be laid on the church to stop the deterioration. In 1924, Father Ramón Mastres restored one of the rooms of the *convento* as a memorial to the early missionaries. Father Mastres hired a local sculptor named Jo Mora to create a life-size bronze figure of Serra on his deathbed. The figures of Fray Crespí, Fray Lasuén, and Fray Julian Lopez (another missionary in Alta California) surround Serra's bed.

Restoration efforts continued, and in 1931 Sir Henry "Harry" John Downie was appointed curator of restoration by Monsignor Philip Scher, the head of the Royal Presidio Chapel in Monterey. Downie began restoring broken statues in the church. During the next 50 years, Downie lowered the front courtyard to stop the church from flooding after each rain, replaced the shingled roof with tiles, and uncovered the original cross in the garth. Using documents written by Fray Palóu in 1784, Downie was able to recreate Fray Serra's room, the library, and the kitchen located in the northeast corner of the *convento*. This area now serves as a museum.

*Jo Mora's sculpture of Fray Serra ▶
surrounded by three other friars.*

The Mission Today

The Church

The mission church was restored to its original state. To recreate the original look, the church was decorated with brightly colored designs and artwork. To make the paints, pigments from minerals were mixed with cactus juice or linseed oil. The painted designs in the church at Mission San Carlos Borromeo had been mostly floral or geometric shapes. The ceiling of the church had a floral design. Now, half-circle patterns are painted on the arched roof supporting the choir loft. Also, triangles of green and white form a pattern along the side walls of the church.

In 1956, Downie replicated the church's original altar. The altar is the centerpiece of the church. It is a table or stand used in Christian religious ceremonies to give offerings to God. The altar table Downie carved has a depiction of the Lamb of God, which represents Christ. Above the altar is a *santo* (painting or sculpture) of St. Charles Borromeo made in Mexico in 1791. In 1961, Pope John XXIII designated the church as a minor basilica, an honor that elevates its status as a house of worship.

The church is also an important burial site. Below the sanctuary floor are the graves of the early mission fathers, including Fray Serra, Fray Crespí, Fray Lopez, and Fray Lasuén.

The *Convento*

Originally, the *convento* surrounding the garth was used as housing for the missionaries and visitors to the mission. Many rooms along the quadrangle's corridor were used as workshops to teach the Esselen

◀ *A view of the mission church.*

49

◀ The mission library.

crafts, such as soapmaking or candlemaking, or to instruct them about Christianity. Today, the southern section of the *convento* is used as an elementary school called the Junípero Serra Catholic School.

The Library

Mission San Carlos Borromeo is the site of California's first library. Originally the library contained only the books that Fray Serra brought with him on his first journey to Alta California in 1769. By 1820, nearly 2,000 books were housed in the mission's library.

The *Camposanto*

In its initial construction, each mission had a *camposanto* (cemetery) near the church. Today at Mission San Carlos Borromeo, the cemetery contains the graves of more than 2,000 Spaniards and Christian Indians who died within the mission complex between 1771 and 1833. The graves are marked by abalone shells laid around mounds of earth. A cross stands to honor their memory.

◀ The church's altar.

Modern-Day Monterey Peninsula

The Monterey Peninsula has continued to thrive since Mission San Carlos Borromeo was founded there. The harvesting of sardines, first begun by the Esselen, became a major industry along Monterey's Cannery Row. The presidio at Monterey is now home to two important schools: the U.S. Naval Postgraduate School and the Defense

▲
This tall cross stands beside the mission church.

Language Institute. The Royal Presidio Chapel has continued to serve as a parish church since its founding in 1794. Today, the coastline between Monterey and Carmel is filled with resorts and golf courses, including the famous Pebble Beach.

Mission San Carlos Borromeo del Río Carmelo is now one of the most popular religious sites in the United States. Visitors come from around the world to tour the restored mission complex. Even Pope John Paul II visited the mission when he came to the United States in 1987.

The Alta California missions have had a major impact on California's economy. The work begun by the missionaries and the American Indians more than two centuries ago has made California the leader in agricultural production in the United States. Moreover, the missions have molded the cultural and historical identity of the state. Mission San Carlos Borromeo reminds visitors and residents of the Carmel Valley of the struggles and hardships that made California what it is today.

Make Your Own Mission
San Carlos Borromeo del Río Carmelo

To make your own model of Mission San Carlos Borromeo del Río Carmelo, you will need:

Supplies:

20" x 20" piece of foamcore
one large piece of cardboard
reddish-brown paint
green and white paint
glue

colorful tissue paper
uncooked lasagna
X-Acto knife
pins

Directions

Step 1: Cut two 8.5" by 10" pieces of foamcore for the front and back of the church.

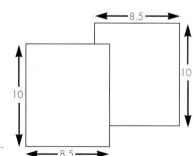

Adult supervision is suggested.

Step 2: Take one of these pieces and cut out windows and a rounded doorway.

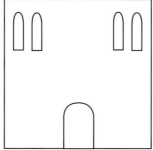

Step 3: At the top of the front of the church, cut the foamcore in the shape of a dome.

Step 4: Cut two 4" by 10" pieces of foamcore for the sides of the church building.

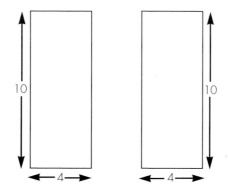

Step 5: Glue the front, back, and side walls of the church together. Stick the walls together with pins until the glue dries.

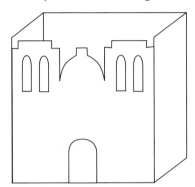

Step 6: Cut four 9″ by 5″ foamcore pieces for the front and back walls of the quadrangle buildings.

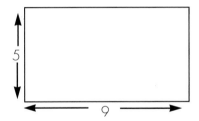

Step 7: Cut two 3″ by 5″ pieces of foamcore for the side walls of the mission quadrangle buildings.

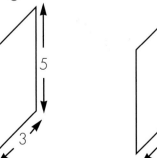

Step 8: Make the quadrangle buildings by gluing two long pieces to each short piece. Pin them until the glue dries. Each structure will only have three sides.

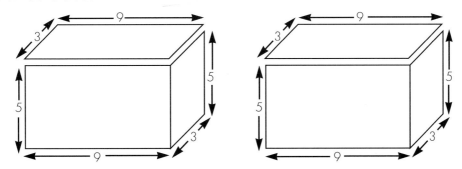

Step 9: Paint the church and the quadrangle buildings light brown, and let dry.

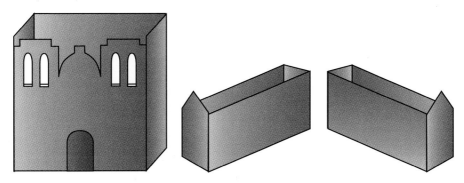

Step 10: Paint the cardboard base green, and let dry.

Step 11: Glue the quadrangle walls to the church. The open space of each rectangle should be attached to one of the side walls of the church. Pin the walls until the glue dries.

Step 12: Glue the church and quadrangle walls to the cardboard base.

Step 13: Paint lasagna noodles reddish-brown and let dry. These will be the tiled roofs of the mission quadrangle walls.

Step 14: Glue the lasagna noodles to the tops of each wall.

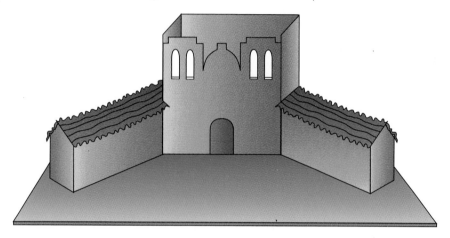

Step 15: Use the tissue paper to make small flowers and trees, and use these to decorate the mission courtyard.

*Use this photo as a reference for building your mission. 57

Important Dates in Mission History

1492	Christopher Columbus reaches the West Indies
1542	Cabrillo's expedition to California
1602	Sebastián Vizcaíno sails to California
1713	Fray Junípero Serra is born
1769	Founding of San Diego de Alcalá
1770	**Founding of San Carlos Borromeo del Río Carmelo**
1771	Founding of San Antonio de Padua and San Gabriel Arcángel
1772	Founding of San Luis Obispo de Tolosa
1775–76	Founding of San Juan Capistrano
1776	Founding of San Francisco de Asís
1776	Declaration of Independence is signed
1777	Founding of Santa Clara de Asís
1782	Founding of San Buenaventura
1784	Fray Serra dies
1786	Founding of Santa Bárbara Virgen y Mártir
1787	Founding of La Purísima Concepción de Maria Santísima
1791	Founding of Santa Cruz and Nuestra Señora de la Soledad
1797	Founding of San José, San Juan Bautista, San Miguel Arcángel, and San Fernando Rey de España
1798	Founding of San Luis Rey de Francia
1804	Founding of Santa Inés Virgen y Mártir
1817	Founding of San Rafael Arcángel
1823	Founding of San Francisco de Solano
1849	Gold found in northern California
1850	California becomes the 31st state

Glossary

adobe (ah-DOH-bee) Sun-dried bricks made of straw, mud, and sometimes manure.

Alta California (AL-tuh kal-ih-FOR-nyuh) The area where the Spanish settled missions, today known as the state of California.

Baja California (BAH-ha kal-ih-FOR-nyuh) The Mexican peninsula directly south of the state of California.

baptize (BAP-tyz) A ceremony performed when someone accepts the Christian faith, intended to cleanse the convert of his sins.

Christian (KRIS-chin) Someone who follows the Christian religion, or the teachings of Jesus Christ and the Bible.

convert (kun-VURT) To change religious beliefs.

diarist (DY-uh-rist) Someone who keeps a record of events.

emancipate (ih-MAN-sih-payt) To give freedom to.

Esselen (EHS-ul-len) American Indians who lived in the Carmel area when the Spanish first arrived in California.

garth (GARTH) A courtyard within the walls of a mission, usually surrounded by the *convento*.

New Spain (NOO SPAYN) The area where the Spanish colonists had their capital in North America, and that would later become Mexico.

sanctuary (SANK-choo-war-ee) A sacred part of a church containing the altar.

secularization (sek-yoo-lur-ih-ZAY-shun) When the operation of the mission lands was turned over to the Christian Indians.

thatch (THACH) Twigs, grass, and bark bundled together.

Pronunciation Guide

asistencia (a-sis-TEN-see-uh)

atole (ah-TOH-lay)

camposanto (kam-po-SAN-toh)

carretas (kah-REH-tahs)

convento (kahn-VEN-toh)

fiesta (fee-EHS-tah)

fray (FRAY)

pozole (poh-ZOH-lay)

ranchería (ran-che-REE-uh)

santo (SAN-toh)

siesta (see-EHS-tah)

vaqueros (ba-KEHR-ohs)

Resources

To learn more about the missions of California, check out these books and Web sites:

Books:

Boulé, Mary Null. *Mission San Carlos Borromeo de Carmelo*. Vashon, WA: Merryant Publishing, 1988.

Lyngheim, Linda. *The Indians and the California Missions*. Van Nuys, CA: Langtry Publications, 1990.

Mission San Carlos Borromeo. Carmel, CA: Carmel Mission Gift Shop, [pamphlet].

Web Sites:

California History for Parents and Teachers:
   http://www.jspub.com

California Missions Resource Page:
   http://www.csd.k12.ca.us/coyote_canyon/4/missions

Mission San Carlos Borromeo:
   http://www.carmelmission.org

Index